17 Top Secrets for How to Keep Your Job or Find New Work Today

17 Top Secrets for How to Keep Your Job or Find New Work Today

by Gini Graham Scott, Ph.D.

Author of a Dozen Books on Work and Professional Development, including *Want It, See It, Get It!* and *Enjoy! 101 Little Ways to Add Fun to Your Work Everyday*

WWW.GINIGRAHAMSCOTT.COM

ASJA Press
New York   Bloomington

**17 Top Secrets for How to Keep Your
Job or Find New Work Today**

ASJA Press
an imprint of iUniverse, Inc.

iUniverse books may be ordered through booksellers or by contacting:

iUniverse
1663 Liberty Drive
Bloomington, IN 47403
www.iuniverse.com
1-800-Authors (1-800-288-4677)

Because of the dynamic nature of the Internet, any Web addresses or links contained in this book may have changed since publication and may no longer be valid.

ISBN: 978-1-4401-4425-7 (pbk)

Printed in the United States of America

iUniverse rev. date: 5/13/2009

CONTENTS

OVERVIEW

17 TOP SECRETS FOR HOW TO KEEP YOUR JOB OR FIND NEW WORK TODAY provides powerful guidelines for how to keep your job or find new work in today's difficult times. It includes a discussion of how to reinvent or remake yourself for the new economy, as well as techniques to relieve stress and enjoy yourself more on or off the job, so you keep up your spirits -- so necessary in these times of turmoil. Techniques on improving your relationships with others are included, too, since these skills are invaluable for staying on the job or finding new work.

The main topics covered, include the following. Feel free to skip around to different chapters, depending on what's most important to you now.
- Keeping your current job – whether you like it or not
- Finding work – or better work
- Finding and creating business opportunities
- Networking to find work, new business opportunities, or just have fun
- Finding ways to be happy – or happier, despite the stresses in your life
- Improving relationships and communications with others

Each of these topics is a section in the book, and each section features several short chapters, which you can easily read. They are ideal when you are traveling, waiting for a job interview, or meeting a prospective new client. They're great to help you feel even more confident and clear about what you want.

Some of these secrets have been adapted from published articles which were originally developed in response to questions from journalists and everyday individuals. Now for the first time, they are collected into a single book as a powerful guide to help you keep your job or find new work and business opportunities.

They are organized into these sections and chapters:

PART I: KEEPING YOUR CURRENT JOB
- Adapting to Changed Conditions
- How to Stick It Out When You Hate Your Boss or Job

PART II: FINDING WORK
- How to Find a Job When You Already Have One
- Volunteering Your Way to a New Job
- How to Find or Create More Work for Yourself
- Using Visualization on the Job Hunt
- Developing New Skills for New Jobs

PART III: FINDING AND CREATING BUSINESS OPPORTUNITIES
- Bartering Instead of Going Bust
- Setting Up a Successful Home-Based Business

PART IV: BUILDING RELATIONSHIPS FOR SUCCESS
- How to Fix Communication Breakdowns
- Networking for the Newly Unemployed

PART V: PROMOTING AND MARKETING YOURSELF
- Creating Your Own Website
- Using the Social Media to Find Work

PART VI: ENJOYING YOURSELF TO GAIN SUCCESS
- You Can Be Happy, Even in Difficult Times
- How to Overcome Stress and Thrive in Today's Tough Times
- How to Have a Happier Workday
- How to Create a Fun Environment for Your Co-workers and Employees

ABOUT THE AUTHOR

Gini Graham Scott, Ph.D. is the author of over 50 books and a seminar/workshop leader, specializing in work relationships and professional and personal development.

She has written a dozen books on work relationships, achieving your goals, and enjoying your work and life more, including: *Want It See It, Get It!, Enjoy! 101 Little Things to Do to Add Fun to Your Work Everyday, A Survival Guide for Working with Humans, A Survival Guide for Working With Bad Bosses, A Survival Guide to Managing Employees from Hell,* and *Disagreements, Disputes, and All-Out War* – all from AMACOM. A number of her books have dealt with management topics, including: *Work with Me! Resolving Everyday Conflicts in Your Organization* (Davies-Black) and *Building a Winning Sales Team* (Probus).

She has a Ph.D. in Sociology from the University of California at Berkeley, and MAs in Anthropology, Mass Communications and Organizational/Consumer/Audience Behavior, and Popular Culture and Lifestyles at Cal State East Bay.

She has gotten extensive media interest in her previous books, including appearances on *Good Morning America, Oprah, Montel Williams, CNN,* and hundreds of radio interviews. She has been frequently quoted by the media and has several Web sites for her books on improving work relationships and professional success, including:

- *Enjoy! 101 Little Ways to Add Fun to Your Work Everyday* (www.enjoythebook.com),
- *Want It, See It, Get It* (www.wantitseeitgetit.com),

- *Disagreements, Disputes, and All Out War, A Survival Guide for Working with Humans* (www.workingwithhumans.com),
- *A Survival Guide to Managing Employees from Hell* (www.workingwithhumans.com),
- *A Survival Guide for Working with Bad Bosses* (www.badbosses. net)

The site featuring her books and speaking on work generally is at www. workwithgini.com. Her overall workshop is at www.ginigrahamscott.com.

PART I:
KEEPING YOUR JOB

CHAPTER 1: ADAPTING TO CHANGED CONDITIONS

When conditions change, you've got to change. It can be very disorienting, especially when you have done a particular type of work for many years. You not only feel competent in doing the work, but you have acquired a network of connections that you can use for support or business leads.

But now you may feel the need to start the process all over again, like moving to a new town and seeking a new line of work. And if you're over 40, the change might be especially daunting, since the time when you made your initial career choice may be way in the past. Even if it isn't, you may feel you are up against younger, more nimble competitors, who are more malleable to change. And taking a pay cut to work your way up in a new profession may be demoralizing, too.

LETTING GO OF THE PAST

A first step to adapting is to stop trying to hold on to the past and pining for the way things use to be. You've got to stop the negative thoughts in your head that are telling you that you can't change, that everything is grim and will stay that way, that you don't have the ability to be successful at something else, or whatever you are thinking to put yourself down. You have to say "Stop" again and again, as long as you need to in order to change your self-destructive messages into something that gives you renewed energy and hope.

That's what Jennifer did. She had a cushy job as an editor in a prestigious publishing house, and she loved working with writers, some with powerful high-profile positions. She basked in the glow of their power and felt that rub off on her. But then came the recession and cutbacks in publishing, and after over ten years on the job, she and a dozen other editors and marketing people in the company were gone. For about two weeks she retreated, feeling dispirited and sorry for herself. But soon she bounced back, turning her long-time experience into work as a part-time editor and book consultant for other would-be writers, using a list of personal contacts in the field and ads on Craigslist to launch her new career. If she couldn't work for a traditional publisher anymore, she would use her skills as a freelancer in the changed publishing landscape.

STOPPING THE NEGATIVE MESSAGES

So what can you do to stop the negative messages and replace them with positive ones? Here are some suggestions.

- Create a trigger for yourself as a reminder to turn your attention to something positive. Then, whenever you notice you are saying or thinking about something negative, release the trigger to stop yourself. A trigger might be anything you choose that signals you to stop what you are doing and shift your attention. For instance, you could snap your fingers, tug on a bracelet on your wrist, lower your arm firmly, or say the words "STOP IT NOW" to yourself.

- Take some time each day to do something you really like to do to treat yourself. Some people call this taking "me" time. Whatever it is, spend at least 20-30 minutes each day doing it. Then, when something negative comes into your mind, chase it away by remembering the last time you did something you really liked.

- Do something nice for someone else. The appreciation you get will help you feel good about doing good. And later, when a negative thought comes to mind, think of how you helped someone else and feel the glow of their appreciation once again.

VISUALIZING WHAT YOU WOULD LIKE TO DO

Another powerful way to get rid of negativity is to visualize what you would like to do if you could do anything you wanted. In turn, this approach will help you tune in on how you might remake yourself and feel excited about the emergence of the new you.

In doing this exercise, don't just think about the future by considering possibilities with your logical mind. Instead, get relaxed, preferably in a quiet private place, ask what you would like to do, and let the images come to you. Don't try to force them; just let them flow into your mind.

For example, one man was wavering about whether to stay in a house he had bought and look for work near where he lived or sell the house and move somewhere else. He wasn't sure, but when he did a visualization, he discovered that the strongest, surest imagery occurred when he considered staying, and ultimately, he saw a beautiful house on a hill that looked like it was waiting for him. It was surrounded by people on either side waving for him to come join him. For him this was a symbol that he should stay where he was for now and appreciate the friends he already had. Perhaps he might even use them to help him get leads in return for a 10% commission on what he made.

ADAPTING TO THE FUTURE

Once the negativity is under control, you can focus on adapting in the future. Some ways to do this include:

- Notice trends in jobs in your area and in parts of the U.S. where you are willing to move. You can get this information from articles in business magazines or try a search on the Internet. (For example, put in the keyword "job trends" or "work trends."

- Identify those trends that are most related to the type of work you have done or would like to do.

- Ask yourself how the work you have done or would like to do could fulfill the requirements of that job. Though you can do this process analytically, use visualization or mental imagery to get a more powerful, emotional hit as you clearly see that job you want – and you can draw on this power to show your enthusiasm for doing the new job.

- Treat finding a job or more clients like a numbers game, where you dedicate 1 or 2 hours a day to marketing yourself, and steel yourself for a lot of rejection. Use the salesperson mantra: "Each no brings me closer to a yes." By thinking in this upbeat way, you put a positive spin on any turn down and don't take it personally – so you are more psyched up to continue going on.

- Try doing some new work as an intern or volunteer to gain new skills. Be willing to work in this new field for a lower amount, and gradually increase the amount of money you are asking for as your skills and experience increase.

- Tell everyone you know that you are looking for a job or clients in this new field, and be ready with flyers they can review for more information. Offer a 10% referral fee as an incentive to more aggressively notice opportunities that might be right for you.

CHAPTER 2:
HOW TO STICK IT OUT
WHEN YOU HATE YOUR
BOSS OR JOB

What do you do if you don't like your job or boss, and you are afraid to strike out on your own, since you fear not finding another job? It's a question that is being asked more and more, as companies downsize and outsource in difficult times.

The easy answer is to stick it out and cope as best you can. But how do you do this? What should you do to make it more bearable to stay on the job when you'd like to be anywhere else?

That's the question that Cynthia had to answer when she hated dealing with her boss each day. She felt he was disorganized and a poor communicator. He frequently changed his mind and then commonly blamed employees for making mistakes for doing "A" when he had decided to change course and do "B." Cynthia felt increasingly frustrated, but didn't want to take a chance on quitting, particularly if that meant getting a poor recommendation which might hamper an already difficult job search.

What to Do If You Dislike Your Boss or Your Job

Here are some suggestions on what to do if you find yourself in that situation of disliking your boss or job and you don't want to quit.

- Create a support group for yourself at work. If you don't like your work situation, you may find that other employees feel similarly. But be discrete when you do this – approach co-workers you feel the closest to and feel you can trust. Even sharing with one other co-worker might help. Or to expand the group, you each might approach another co-worker in the same way. Once you find a buddy or support group, find a time when you can comfortably get together, preferably off the job, such as during lunch or after work. Then, as you share your gripes, you'll realize you aren't alone. And as a group, you might even be able to come up with ways to improve the situation, such as providing a poor communicator boss with input on what you each are doing, so you can do a better job.

- Look for ways to individually or as a group improve the situation. For example, if a boss is disorganized and unclear about what he or she wants you to do, take the initiative in clarifying what he or she wants. One way is writing down your understanding of what you think your boss wants; another way is asking to talk to your boss and explaining your understanding of what you are supposed to do. Choose a method of your communication that your boss prefers, such as whether to write a memo or have a meeting.

- Seek to mentally and emotionally accept your situation, so you feel better about what you are doing, even if you don't like doing it. Then, as you work on experiencing acceptance, you may find you really do feel better about your job – and your more positive attitude might make your boss and others respond more positively to you. For example, suppose you feel your boss is being overbearing in supervising you too closely, which makes you feel tense and anxious. You might try some self-talk where you remind yourself that this is how things are and you have to accept what is; you have to go along to get along; you have to learn to "suck it up" as they say. Though seeking such acceptance may not be an ideal situation, tell yourself again and again that it's not worth fighting against the way things are; instead it's better to accept, ACCEPT, ACCEPT! For an even more powerful experience of this realization, relax in a quiet, private place and visualize the word "ACCEPT" vibrating through your mind and visualize yourself in a scene where you are being humble and accepting. In short, find a way to persuade yourself to accept what you can't change. Or as the well-known expression goes: "God grant me the serenity to accept the things I cannot change, the courage to change the things I can, and the wisdom to know the difference."

- Find some things to do that you enjoy doing after work, so you have something pleasant to think about and enjoy while on the job. Or if you have a routine job you can perform on automatic, let your mind roam freely. Or during a break, imagine something that you really like to do.

- Look for ways to make your environment in the office more pleasant, so you have things you like to look at or think about, so you enjoy your work more. For instance, if you are allowed to do this, put pictures on the wall of your office or find fun objects to put on your desk. In turn, other co-workers may do the same, creating a more pleasant environment for all. Or your pictures and objects can become a conversation starter, drawing you closer to others in the office. And maybe your boss may become easier to work with, too.

In short, if you have to stick it out, find ways to make sticking around more acceptable and enjoyable. And in so doing you may find you go from sticking it out because you feel stuck to being glad you stuck around.

PART II: FINDING WORK

CHAPTER 3:
HOW TO FIND A JOB
WHEN YOU ALREADY
HAVE ONE

You're in a stronger position to find a job if you already have one, and in today's work environment, it's better to hang on to a current job, even if you don't like your job or your boss, while you look. However, be careful when you do so to avoid others at work – and especially your boss – knowing that you are looking.

Here are some tips on how to strategically look for a job while you have one without getting found out.

MANAGING E-MAILS

- Do not send e-mails about other jobs from your work computer, even if you are on your own time for a lunch break or before or after work. Someone might easily see your e-mails, particularly your boss, who may periodically monitor workplace computers to see what people are doing.
- Use your home computer or bring a laptop to work for sending out any e-mail queries during the day.

BEING CAREFUL WHO YOU TELL

- Don't talk about your frustrations on the job or your plans to get another to any other employees, even if you feel they can be trusted. People can talk and the word can get around.

- Limit the number of friends and associates you tell about your job search and only tell those who you feel you can trust to maintain your confidence and who might be sources of referrals to job leads. When you do tell them, ask them not to mention you or your job search to anyone else.

PRESERVING YOUR PRIVACY

- Avoid publicly complaining or bad-mouthing the company you currently work for. The word may get around that you are dissatisfied, raising suspicions that you are looking for a job
- Use another name when you make initial calls to learn about job opportunities. Then if there is a job opening, you can use your real name when you submit your application in confidence.

STAYING ON THE JOB

- Continue to do your current job, even if you don't like it, with energy and enthusiasm, so your boss and co-workers continue to see you as a hard-working employee and good team player. That way you will be more likely to keep your current job – and get a good reference when you do leave.

CHAPTER 4:
VOLUNTEERING YOUR
WAY TO A NEW JOB

At networking parties for the film industry and the unemployed – sometimes the same people in both groups -- I have been running into a growing number of people who speak desperately about spending 30 or 40 hours a week sending out resumes and trying to set up interviews. But then, nothing. There are no jobs. So their job has become finding a job – though there are few jobs at a time when layoffs are spreading from industry to industry. No wonder they are increasingly depressed.

THE BENEFITS OF VOLUNTEERING

Sometimes if you are faced with such a situation, the best approach is to give up a frustrating and fruitless job search for now. Instead, think about how you can volunteer to do something where the work is needed and where your skills and interests make this task a good fit. Volunteering is a good way to learn new skills, as well as keep you busy and fulfilled, because you are making a contribution. Later you can use that experience to help you get a paying job – or get clients to pay you for using these skills on their behalf.

As an example of the value of volunteering, I just read a *People* magazine article about Mary Marzano, 49, of Maplewood, New Jersey, whose sister's home in Galveston was destroyed by Hurricane Ike. Mary discovered from a hotel-employee friend that the hotel threw out sheets and towels each month in order to provide the guests with new linens. Realizing that the poor people in Galveston could use the sheets and towels, Mary began collecting them from local hotels and shipping dozens of boxes of sheets to the stricken area.

Then, she began sending these extra linens, along with donated quilts and bathrobes, to local charities and public services, including Goodwill, the Salvation Army, and some homeless shelters.

Though Mary has been doing this mission of good will on weekends, since she works as an advertising-account supervisor, she has developed a skill she could now use to find a new job or create a business for herself, say as a project manager. Likewise, you might do such volunteer work during the work week, when you are out of work with little hope of a paid job in sight, and later use the new skills and contacts to gain paid work.

GETTING STARTED AS A VOLUNTEER

So where should you volunteer? One approach is to look through the listings of local organizations in your areas seeking volunteers. Another is to create your own volunteer activity, as Mary did, where you find a need and fill it. Note the skills you use as a volunteer and keep track of the people you meet along the way.

Then, look for people who have projects or part-time work using that skill. Or you may be able to turn your volunteer work into a paid job, once the organization is ready to hire again. And later, when the economy revives and there are new job openings, you have a whole new repertoire of skills to offer. And prospective employers will like your altruistic, can-do spirit, increasing your chances of getting a paying job.

CHAPTER 5:
HOW TO FIND OR
CREATE MORE WORK
FOR YOURSELF

Even with the new hope inspired by Obama's program to stimulate the economy and can do attitude, pragmatic reality is setting in, as more and more banks and stores are affected by the recession, and the unemployment rate rises. Most recently, it was up to over 10% in California, about 8% throughout the country.

However, deep recessions can prove to be a land of opportunity, since many people who can't find work are looking for other ways to make money. Thus, this can be a better time than ever to think about your skills, what people need today, and find a fit between what you offer and these needs. For example, hundreds of new entrepreneurs have been launching Internet start-ups, with limited up-front costs and high potential, such as writing an e-book with a topic people want to know about today, like how to make money on the Internet.

FINDING NEW OPTIONS IN TODAY'S ECONOMY

So what might you do to appeal to today's market? Think of start-up possibilities you could launch yourself -- or look into direct sales programs you could represent with products or services people might need and want. But be cautious of scammers promising riches through pyramid schemes. Look for companies with solid products or services that people really do want to buy, aside from any money making opportunities. Since so many people are out of work now, this is an especially good time for starting a new business with talented people you can employ at lower than usual starting wages.

In short, if you can't find work for yourself now, consider creating your own company and work opportunity for others. As Charles Dickens once said -- "It was the best of times, it was the worst of times...it was the season of Light, it was the season of Darkness, it was the spring of hope, it was the winter of despair." Well, this is all of these things now, but if you choose, you can make it "the best of times, the season of Light, and the spring of hope."

KEY QUESTIONS TO DECIDE WHAT TO DO

So take some time to ask yourself some questions to decide what you want to do to make the best choices for you:

- What kind of skills and talents do I have? List your strongest ones and prioritize by ranking them from 1 (highest) to 5 (lowest) which you would most like to use now?
- What do people especially need now that they aren't getting from other companies or individuals?
- How can I apply my skills and talents to provide products or services that will help others fulfill their needs and wants? Do this for each of your top skills and talents first; then go on to the next highly ranked group for still more ideas.
- What steps can I take to develop, promote, and provide these products and services? Create a list of steps to take.
- What do I need to put these steps into action, such as employees, materials, or contacts with other companies or individuals?
- Finally, put these steps into action. Start now by taking the first step.

CHAPTER 6:
USING VISUALIZATION
ON THE JOB HUNT

Using visualization can be a powerful tool to help you land a job – or create work assignments for yourself as an alternative to finding a job.

It may be that your field has been undergoing lay-offs or restructuring, so you can't find the kind of job you have had in the past. If so, think about how the skills and talents you have can be applied in a new setting. Or think about what new skills you need to learn for something you would like to do. Or instead of finding a new job, you might turn your skills into a service you can provide.

Visualization can help by enabling you to imagine the possibilities, so you can come up with more ideas to choose from and then feel more strongly and knowingly what to do. In a sense, finding a job or creating new work for yourself in today's tough times takes more imagination and creativity. But if you put your power of visualization to work, you can do this more successfully.

GETTING STARTED IN USING THE
VISUALIZATION PROCESS

To prepare for the visualization process, get some paper and a pen to write with, so you can note your great ideas. Or use a recording device, if you would prefer to say your ideas aloud rather than write them. Then, find a comfortable quiet place where you can be alone for about 20-30 minutes.

Now get relaxed and imagine there is a screen in front of you where you will see the answers in the form of images or words in your mind's eye. Then, ask yourself a series of questions and don't try to judge or rate the answers in any way. You'll do that later, when it comes time to prioritize and choose.

KEY QUESTIONS TO ASK TO HELP YOUR JOB SEARCH

Now ask yourself the following questions as relevant to your job search. I mentioned some of these in the previous chapter on how to find or create more work for yourself, but they are so critical, they are worth repeating.

- What kind of skills and talents do I have? Just write down or record whatever comes to mind. Later, you can rate your strongest skills and prioritize by ranking them from 1 (highest) to 5 (lowest) which you would most like to use now?
- What types of industries might be able to use my job skills? Again, just write down or record whatever comes to you, and later you can rate the industries you prefer and prioritize them.
- What steps can I take now to approach people in these industries about a new job?
- How can I best present myself to offer these job skills?
- What new skills might I develop which are needed now? How can I develop these skills as quickly as possible?
- What might I do to show that I can apply these new skills in this new field?

Then, based on the type of job you are looking for and your skills that are relevant to this job, show how you can apply these skills, such as by creating a portfolio to show what you can do. Also, get testimonials from individuals or organizations where you have used these skills as a volunteer.

KEY QUESTIONS TO ASK TO CREATE A NEW BUSINESS

If you are open to creating a new business using your skills and talents, ask yourself the following questions:

- What do people especially need now that they aren't getting from other companies or individuals?
- How can I apply my skills and talents to providing products or services to help others fulfill their needs and wants? Do this for

each of your top skills and talents first; then go on to the next highly ranked group for still more ideas.

- What steps can I take to develop, promote, and provide these products and services? Create a list of steps to take.
- What do I need to put these steps into action, such as employees, materials, and contacts with other companies or individuals?
- Finally, put these steps into action. Start now by taking the first step.

THE ADVANTAGES OF USING VISUALIZATION TECHNIQUES

The advantage of using visualization techniques as you ask these questions is that you tap into your intuition or the creative force within you. So you don't just think of but see and experience the answers. This way you can come up with more and better ideas, and you can better see what to do to turn these ideas into action.

CHAPTER 7:
DEVELOPING NEW
SKILLS FOR NEW JOBS

Suppose you need to develop new skills to change your career path, since the opportunities have declined in your old career -- or maybe your past line of work has become irrelevant in a transforming economy. Some examples of this dramatic transformation are the store clerk, manager, or owner in a video store, which is being made obsolete as customers increasingly download content or order their DVDs online. Another profession with diminishing returns is the travel agent, who is being replaced by online ticketing and individual consumers checking online sites like Expedia for travel bargains.

So how do you develop new skills or even know what skills to develop? A first step is doing a skills assessment, discussed in Chapters 5 and 6, to look at your strengths and weaknesses. Then, look at employment trends and want ads to see where there might be a good fit for you with new jobs that involve the skills you have identified. Keep a tally of the ads you see to help you clearly see which types of jobs are offered the most and the terms used to describe these new jobs.

Then, having decided what new skills you need to develop, the next step is making arrangements to develop them. Some possibilities include:

- Take a class at a local community college or university extension program which offers a training program in the selected skill.

- Look for local organizations and online groups offering training in these skills. Try searching in Google or Yahoo by putting in the name of the skills you want to develop and your city or neighboring cities for local groups. Or join a group that connects people with like interests, such as www. meetup.com, which is a national organization, where many organizers post workshops, seminars, and training programs.

- Volunteer to work for an organization or company that is doing work in an area you want to get into, so you can acquire the basic skills and practice using them. Then, when you feel comfortable with these new skills, seek jobs where you will use them. Be willing to start at a lower salary or consulting level than you are used to, which will help you get in the door, as you face others who are more experienced than you. Though you may lack more extensive experience, your willingness to learn and grow, shown by your internship and any courses you have taken, may help you land the job.

- Join or create a support group for others who are learning the new skills you are developing. You can practice together or provide each other with assistance and motivation to keep learning the new skill. It can sometimes seem daunting when you feel there is so much to learn and so many skilled people are so far ahead of you. But having a support group behind you can help you to keep working on honing your skills – you are not alone, because you have the encouragement of others in the group.

PART III: FINDING AND CREATING BUSINESS OPPORTUNITIES

CHAPTER 8:
BARTERING INSTEAD OF
GOING BUST

Bartering is a system of trade that predates the use of money, whereby you trade your skills, services, or products for something you want from someone else.

About 25 years ago, during a recession in the early 1980s, numerous bartering clubs sprang up, so people who were out of work or having financial problems could increase the funds available to them. Once people joined the group, they could turn their skills, services or products into points; then others could employ them or purchase their products using the points they had accumulated in their own accounts. And if no one wanted their offerings, they would accumulate negative points up to a cap, until they found a way to share what they offered. Through this system, these clubs sought to achieve a fair balance between what people were getting and giving.

Back then, I met several people at business and networking groups who had organized these systems, and for a small amount of real money, people could join. Though I didn't join myself, not needing the extra cash at the time, I met many people who found these systems of great value, as well as the entrepreneurs who set them up. Then, as the economy recovered, interest in these bartering clubs declined and many closed as people rejoined the mainstream economy.

This seems to be a good approach to renew today, whether you organize a bartering system or join one.

ORGANIZING A BARTER SERVICE

As an organizer, think of running a barter service as a new business, which can be very successful if you have the skills needed to run the business, such as a good head for figures, an attention to detail for everyday operations, and good communication, marketing, and sales skills to promote the service. You will also need a minimal number of people with different skills in your local area, so members can offer a wide range of skills, products, and services for an exchange.

PARTICIPATING IN A BARTER SERVICE

If you simply want to participate in bartering, you can do this directly by offering an exchange with your own contacts or try posting your offerings on one of the social media sites like Linked In. You can also tell people in your list of e-mail contacts what you are offering and what you want. Or join a bartering service to list your skills, services, and products, and describe what you hope to gain in exchange.

To determine what to list, think about what you have done in the past and list what you can offer that might interest someone else. If you have a lot to offer, divide up your skills, services, or products by category, and post them separately.

CHAPTER 9: SETTING UP A SUCCESSFUL HOME-BASED BUSINESS

In these difficult times, more and more people are setting up home-based businesses. To do so yourself, here are some steps to optimize your chances for success.

SETTING UP A SPACE IN YOUR HOME

- Set up a dedicated space in your home for your work, where you can close the door, so you feel like you are going to work – and anyone else in your house will know this.
- Equip your work area with the necessary materials for your type of business. Visualize what you are going to be doing on a day-to-day basis, and create a list for what you need. Pare it down to the basic essentials if you have a limited budget. When you go shopping, look for store specials, no-interest loans for purchases, discounts, and other retail incentives to keep down your costs.

SETTING PLACE AND TIME BOUNDARIES

- Create some boundaries with your family and friends, so they know you are working at certain times and don't distract you with non-work calls or questions. Explain that they should regard this work time and work space for that purpose only, as if you were going to work in the office.

ORGANIZING YOURSELF TO BE MORE EFFECTIVE

- Work out a schedule for when you will be checking your e-mails, such as every two or three hours, so you can concentrate on your work between making e-mail checks. Let people know that if something is crucial and needs fast action to call you; otherwise they should contact you by e-mail. This way, you cut down on the distractions from too frequent e-mail checks and phone calls, so you have a solid block of time to work.
- Dedicate about 2-3 hours a day for marketing your product or service, including going to networking events.

CREATING A WEBSITE FOR YOUR BUSINESS

- Set up a Website for your business which looks professional. To keep your costs down, you can use a hosting service offering templates, such as Sitebuilder, where you can choose from several hundred Website formats; then customize it for your business. This way you don't have to start from scratch to build your Website.
- Feature the products or services you want to sell on your Website and make it easy to buy them, such as by setting up Amazon or Paypal payment account, so people can easily click and pay. If possible, set up a merchant account with your bank, so people can pay you by credit cards, too.

USING PROMOTIONAL MATERIALS

- Create flyers, brochures, or catalog sheets about your products or services, and take some of them with you wherever you go, so you can give them out as appropriate to people you meet at networking events, business expos, or in your day to day activities.
- Look for opportunities to turn the conversation to what you are marketing; then if people are interested, give out your flyers, brochures, catalog sheets, or a business card, which includes your Website and email. You can order these materials inexpensively through a number of Internet companies, such as Vista Prints.

PART IV: BUILDING RELATIONSHIPS FOR SUCCESS

CHAPTER 10:
HOW TO FIX
COMMUNICATION
BREAKDOWNS

Communication breakdowns often occur because people don't say something or because of the way they say it. Here are some tips for overcoming these communication breakdowns:

SHOWING INTEREST OR EXPLAINING WHEN YOU ARE BUSY

- If you sound rushed and distracted when you say something, people may think you are not interested or feel offended, because it seems like they are unimportant to you.
- If you are rushed, provide the other person with a brief explanation that you are very busy with something now, but want to talk with that person later, so either you or they can contact you again.

AVOIDING FALSE ASSUMPTIONS

- Often breakdowns occur because someone has false assumptions about someone or about something they expect someone to do; then they communicate based on those assumptions.
- For example, a boss or co-worker assumes you already know something or you will take on a particular role or responsibility, when you don't expect to do so. In this case, it is best to confirm

in a conversation, memo or e-mail what you expect someone to do or what you understand they want you to do. Then, if they don't understand something the same way, they should tell you or you can clarify the matter yourself, so you are both on the same page.

GAINING CLARIFICATION WHERE NECESSARY

- Another reason for a communication breakdown is that someone doesn't say something or ask for clarification, because they don't want to appear stupid, feel uncomfortable asking or explaining something, or want to be diplomatic by not bringing up a subject that might make others uncomfortable. Or sometimes a person doesn't want to admit he or she wasn't listening or didn't understand something, and hopes to figure it out later.
- When there is such a breakdown, the best approach is to make the other person feel comfortable and safe to ask questions, even if s/he thinks s/he should know that. Conversely, if you are unsure or unclear about something, ask. If the boss seems hard to approach, try asking a co-worker. Or feed back what you do understand and invite the other person to fill in what h/she wants you to do.

LISTENING TO OTHERS

- Communication breakdowns also occur when people don't allow time for others to ask questions or don't take time to listen carefully to others. For example, a boss gives everyone instructions on what to do, but not everyone understands. Or an employee doesn't listen closely when instructions are given. In this case, make sure everyone has understood what you have just explained and invite them to ask questions if they don't understand something. Another approach is to invite someone to provide a brief recap of what they think you said.
- Conversely, if you are listening to instructions, actively engage your mind so you really listen. Imagine yourself doing what you will be doing, as the other person talks. Afterwards, be ready to ask for clarification or for examples of what to do if there is anything you don't understand.

CHAPTER 11: NETWORKING FOR THE NEWLY UNEMPLOYED

Since layoffs have been increasing, a new type of networking is emerging that echoes the pink slip parties held during the dot.com bust -- though now unemployment has been hitting just about every type of industry. Besides pink slip parties, there are a growing number of unemployed groups forming all over, where people can provide each other with support, job tips, help with resume writing, and more.

GROUPS FOR THE UNEMPLOYED

One such group is the Unemployed Social Network, which, with some irony, was started by the founder of the Future Millionaires of Santa Monica. However, after getting little response to the Future Millionaires and a growing response to the Unemployed group, including a feature on a local news show, the founder, Jeremy Erickson, decided to focus on building the unemployed group. And he has found his own niche in serving the unemployed market -- by writing resumes. He has invited meeting participants to bring their resumes, cover letters, and portfolios to work on them to make them better, and has announced his availability as a coach and mentor to help.

He has also suggested a series of rules for getting employed. Among them: "Get off your butts...talk to people...build a great looking resume...network, network, network...and send out as many resumes as you can per day." He advises playing the numbers game, which means making as many calls and contacts as you can to set up meetings, since you increase your chances that something will come through. It's the approach successful salespeople use in considering that every "no" means you are getting closer to getting a "yes."

Erickson additionally suggests doing what you can to stand out to get the attention of the employer. For example, print your resume on heavier and lightly colored paper or include a color photo of yourself. Finally he says: "Don't lose hope." That way you maintain a positive, upbeat attitude, which helps draw people to you.

Besides these unemployed groups, I've discovered a growing number of business networking and entrepreneur groups, which include many of the unemployed. Often these small businesses and start-ups are a good source of jobs and opportunities, and many of them have been founded by the formerly employed. And all types of groups -- from social to business groups -- are sponsoring pink slip and unemployment parties -- a sign of the times.

Finding and Participating in Groups for the Unemployed

How do you find such groups? Check if you have a local networking group such as MeetUp in your area. If so, put in some relevant search terms, such as "unemployed," "networking," "entrepreneur", and "jobs" to see what groups in that category exist in your area. Another source of such groups is Craigslist. Look for your city or county, and check for community and other types of groups in that location.

Then, start going to these events. Bring business cards, and if you don't have them yet, you can get them made up for about $50 dollars from various online business card printers like Vista Print. Work on a resume highlighting the skills you feel are most salable, along with the jobs that are most relevant. And be ready to adapt your resume to the job you are interviewing for. Just rearrange and change your copy on your computer as appropriate, and keep copies of these different resumes, so you can easily print them up or e-mail them to prospective employers. Keep your resume updated, too, such as if you find a part-time job.

Also, be willing to lower the salary range you are looking for, so you can jump aboard some of the new start-ups that are just leaving the station. They commonly can't afford much pay to start, but many will grow into a powerful engine of the new economy, opening up even more opportunities in the future.

And if you're an employer, particularly in a start-up business or small company, such events are a good way to find well-qualified employees who are willing to start at a lower than usual salary just to be working. I know first hand, because I've gone to such groups to hire a few administrative assistants, and I've quickly gotten dozens of resumes from people eager to work again.

PART V: PROMOTING AND MARKETING YOURSELF

CHAPTER 12: CREATING YOUR OWN WEBSITE

Having your own Website is increasingly important to showcase who you are. While having a presence on LinkedIn, Facebook, and other social media sites can help, having your own Website with your own domain name contributes to your presence and authority.

CREATING AN ONLINE RESUME

You can use your Website for your online resume, and send prospective employers or clients there as an easy alternative to sending them a resume, as they prefer. Another advantage of having a Website is you can present this information to the potential employer or client by giving a link in your initial e-mail, since many people are wary of opening attachments unless requested. So you speed up the process of providing your credentials, without having to wait for a request to send them – which can contribute to getting a decision in your favor more quickly.

When you plan your resume, your visualization abilities can help you decide on the design of the Website and what to include. For example, if you get relaxed and let your intuitive, creative powers guide you, you might see your Website vividly before you, and as you watch, you'll see the categories laid out for you on your mental screen. You can also imagine what to say on your home page and other pages on your Website.

Staying Focused on the Type of Work You Want

Keep your Website focused around the type of work you want to do. Then, this information helps to sell you as an expert or experienced person in this area. If you are looking for two different types of work or business opportunities, it is generally better to have separate Websites, so you can target your appeals to these different markets.

Use your homepage to provide an overview of what you do and the benefits you can offer an employer or client. Include one or two testimonials or recommendations on this page if you have them, and if you have a short video introducing yourself, include this, as well.

Using Links to Provide More Information

Visitors to your Website can go to the appropriate link to learn more. Include these links on your navigation bar or headers, as well as in the copy on your home page. Some key links to include, since you are seeking work, are to a more detailed bio or resume (1-2 pages max), a page of testimonials, and if you've gotten any special rewards or recognition for your work, include a page for that. If you are doing a blog associated with your Website, include a link to that. Finally, include a page with your contact information. Provide a phone number and address as well as an email.

Keeping It Professional

Since this is a professional Website, don't try to be cutesy or humorous and don't include personal highlights, such as pictures of your family or family dog or a description of your favorite hobby. Prospective employers and clients are primarily interested in what you can do for them, so emphasize the benefits you can provide when you work for them.

Getting People to Your Website

Once your Website is set up, let people know about it by including the Website URL in any information you hand out or email to people, such as your resume, brochure, flyer, and business card. Add it to your signature in emails. Should you fill out an application for employment or for references for clients, include it in that.

There are all sorts of ways to entice visitors to come to your Website, such as using SEO (search engine optimization) or a click through advertising campaign. With an SEO campaign, you put keywords in your Website copy for your type of work that are best recognized by the search engines. In a click through advertising campaign, like Google AdWords, you use keywords in your ads to generate traffic. You can use keywords to direct prospective clients in a particular area, such as including the name of your city or county in a phrase in Adwords (such as "lawyer San Francisco")

Or if you generally use social networking and cold calling for your initial contact, use your Website as more of a brochure or online resume, where you send people after they express interest in learning more about your work. Then, your Website helps to validate your credentials and show people why they should hire you.

CHAPTER 13: USING THE SOCIAL MEDIA TO FIND WORK

Have you tweeted anyone on Twitter lately? Do you have a profile on Facebook? Are you connected on LinkedIn? For some types of work and businesses, these and other social media sites can be a way to make connections that can lead to a job or new clients. Or you might get tips and support from others you are connected to.

Besides these three sites, which have the greatest following today, there are numerous other sites – some specific to a particular industry – which can provide these connections. For instance, some others include Grouply, Plaxo, TribeHollywood (for the film industry), and there are many more.

BUILDING CONNECTIONS

The basic way these social media sites work is that you build up direct connections with friends and contacts you know or invite to join you; then you are connected to other people through them. For example, on Twitter, you have followers and follow others; on Facebook, you have friends you communicate with by writing on each other's walls; and on LinkedIn, you have links to other professionals.

GOING FROM CASUAL CONVERSATIONS TO ANNOUNCEMENTS ONLINE

On some social media sites you can announce what you are doing, join in ongoing real time conversations with others, and sign up for interest groups, where you can share information with the entire group. However, avoid blatant publicity and promotions about something, so people don't feel spammed.

Instead, what works well is to gradually build up links, friends, and followers, and let people know what you are doing and comment on what others are doing. You can also offer helpful advice that provides value, so people welcome your input. This way you become part of a community, as well as communicating directly with the people you already know – or have come to know as a group member.

Once you have become a part of these groups, you can send out announcements about what you are doing or what you are looking for, and include a link to your Website (which you should have)for that type of work. Just keep your message short – up to 140 characters max, which is what Twitter allows for its tweets. For instance, you might say something like: "YOUR NAME has just finished training to become a (TYPE OF JOB) or "YOUR COMPANY has just launched a new service helping rescued animals find owners)." As long as you list something that people will find interesting or valuable, they may not only respond themselves, but pass on this information to others.

Special Services to Facilitate Your Messages

Once you have established a presence in more than one of these social media sites, you can use a service to provide updates on your activities in all the major sites where you have an account (and you'll discover other social media sites to check out, too). One such service is www.ping.fm. You designate the social media sites you belong to, put in your message (keeping it under 140 characters), and then ping (send) it. Your message will show up on all of your sites.

So what if your link is to a long Website URL? Well, the Internet has provided a solution to that. Just go to www.tinyurl.com, type in your long URL, and it the site will transform this longer link into a shorter one – typically only about 25 characters.

Assessing the Results

Once you start a social media campaign, be sure to assess how well it is working for you. Allow about 4 to 6 weeks to create a presence, spending about 2-3 hours a day on this. A good first step is to make connections by building up your links. Then, as you continue to build links, gradually start posting messages about the kind of work or clients you can help with, emphasizing the benefits you provide.

Next notice what kind of responses you are getting. Are any of them leading to potential job offers or clients? If not, try tweaking your campaign by changing the messages you are sending out. Also, review your Website. Maybe that could use some tweaking, too. Then, monitor the results over the next week or two.

Finally, assess whether the campaign is working for you. The social media work well for some people, though not for others, but you don't know until you try it. And even if you don't find that a social media campaign works to get you work, you might still find it valuable as a fun way to interact with others online and make new social connections. You never know where this campaign will lead until you try it for awhile.

PART VI:
ENJOYING YOURSELF TO
GAIN SUCCESS

CHAPTER 14: YOU CAN BE HAPPY, EVEN IN DIFFICULT TIMES

As each day brings more and more bad news about the state of the world, you could use an antidote to today's doom and gloom to rejuvenate yourself. What? Try applying the principles of happiness to whatever is happening in your life today, so you can enjoy whatever you are doing and get rid of your feelings of stress.

THE TWELVE PRINCIPLES OF HAPPINESS

The 12 principles of happiness are listed below. Think about them each day, so you regularly apply them; perhaps keep them on a list you see regularly, so they stick in your mind. Eventually, this way of experiencing happiness will become a habit and way of life, so you enjoy every day, no matter what happens. It's an outlook that will help to drive away fear and other negative feelings about work and your economic future.

1. First cultivate **love**, which is often called the "root of happiness" and the polar opposite of fear. To do so, remind yourself to experience and express appreciation for the work, friends, and significant others you have in your life. Focus on what you have now or will have, so you feel gratitude, not on what you don't have or used to have, causing you to feel a sense of loss.

2. Be **optimistic.** To this end, put aside any painful experiences by letting them go or thinking about how you can learn from whatever difficulties you encounter. Optimism can help you overcome any regrets for the past and lead you to feel confident about what the future will bring.

3. Cultivate **courage** by actively embracing challenges as a way to overcome feelings of fear.

4. Remind yourself that you always have the **freedom** to choose whatever the situation. Should you feel stuck where you are, think of the different ways you might remake yourself and do something different; consider how you might adapt your skills to respond to today's economic situation.

5. Be **proactive**, so you shape your own destiny, rather than waiting for other people or events to make you happy. Think about what you can change or do differently to reshape who you are or what you are doing now.

6. Gain **security** by liking and accepting who you are, so you have an inner sense of assurance, since everything else in life is constantly changing. So seek security, which comes from within, not from outer attributes, such as money or popularity.

7. Take steps to protect your **health**, because you need to feel healthy to be happy, while feeling happy will contribute to your good health.

8. Have a sense of **spirituality**, which means being open to experiences beyond your everyday life, whatever your religious faith. This sense of spirituality can help you feel secure and give you a feeling of strength and purpose, so you are better able to weather difficulties you encounter in daily life.

9. Embrace and express **altruism**, since you will gain great satisfaction through giving to others and feeling connected to them; it will help you have a sense of purpose. By contrast, overly self-absorbed people are generally not truly happy.

10. Cultivate a sense of **perspective**, so you are better able to distinguish between big and small problems and prioritize what is more and less important, rather than being rigid. This way you can put your

current difficulties into a larger context. For instance, you might view current economic uncertainties as a time of change preparing you to move on to newer more satisfying work in the future.

11. Look on whatever happens with a sense of **humor**, which will help you lighten up and move past current difficulties.

12. Have a sense of **purpose**, which will give meaning to your life. It will enable you to feel satisfied that you are doing what you were meant to do.

APPLYING THE PRINCIPLES IN YOUR WORK AND PERSONAL LIFE

Now that you know the 12 happiness principles, think about how you might apply them in your work and personal life. You may already be using many of these principles. But now pay attention to how and when you are using them, so you appreciate yourself for what you are already doing – an example of the first principle: love. For you are showing self-love by appreciating yourself.

CHAPTER 15:
HOW TO OVERCOME STRESS AND THRIVE IN TODAY'S TOUGH TIMES

Today, as the financial upheaval spreads through the economy, more and more employees are affected, and those still on the job are experiencing increasing stress. Employees and managers alike are asking themselves if they'll be the next to go, just as company owners are asking the same question of their companies. It's like a survival of the fittest struggle, as employees and managers strive to stay in place and not be ousted.

What can you do to not merely survive but even thrive in these tough times? Here are some suggestions, so you feel less stress whatever happens and are more likely to come out ahead.

WAYS TO RELAX AND OVERCOME STRESS

- Do some relaxation exercises, so you feel less tense and anxious, which will enable you to better cope with everyday activities and perform at your best.
- Notice where the points of tension are at work and think about what you might do to smooth things over, whether that involves talking to someone or taking on extra responsibilities. Then go do it.

The Value of Working Harder and Helping Others

- Be willing to work harder and take on extra responsibilities even if you are not being paid more -- or are being paid less. When things improve again, people will remember and you will reap the rewards accordingly.
- Remind yourself that some other people are more badly affected by the financial meltdown than you, and consider volunteering to help those who are; you'll feel much better for being of service to others.

Seek to Imagine and Get What You Want for the Future

- Create a wish list and imagine you have achieved your wishes. Then, imagine what you might do to achieve them. Just thinking this way will help you not only feel better but put you on the path to getting what you want.

Stay Upbeat and Positive

- Think of what you can do to brighten up your day and others' day at work with some little fun activities. Then, seek to put them in action. You'll help dispel the mood of doom and gloom that pervades many workplaces today, and your initiative can help you not only stay on the job but get ahead at work when the good times come back.

CHAPTER 16: HOW TO HAVE A HAPPIER WORKDAY

Today, even if you don't like your job, you may feel lucky to have it. So how can you brighten up your day so you enjoy your job more? By doing so, you may find you do like your job after all, do better work, and end up getting promoted to an even better job.

Here are some tips on what to do, based on my workshops and interviews with dozens of employees and managers.

WAYS TO RELAX AND FEEL MORE POSITIVE AND UPBEAT

- Do a relaxation exercise or meditation, where you concentrate on what you like about your job. Think about the activities or people you like the most, and keep your focus on them. Make your visualization as vivid as possible, as you imagine yourself doing those activities or being with those people.
- Such exercises or meditation will leave you feeling more positive and upbeat. And as researchers have found, what you think about helps make you more attentive to and aware of those experiences, since we all perceive what is around us selectively, based on the mental schema or perceptual framework we bring with us.

WAYS TO CREATE A MORE POSITIVE ENVIRONMENT

- Fix up your office or desk with objects that are fun and expressive of you. They will not only brighten your day but be great conversation starters. For example, one very popular bank manager who loved purple, not only often wore purple, but she put all sorts of purple items on her desk, from little cars to purple puppies, and she prided herself on being called the "Purple Lady." She not only created a cheerful environment around her, but customers loved her.

- Collect amusing cartoons, jokes, and articles, and post them around your office, desk, or in the lunchroom. You might send them by e-mail, too, before or after work or on breaks, if that's acceptable in your office. These sharings help to create a more playful, comfortable atmosphere for not only you, but for everyone. And they can be conversation starters for lunch and breaks during the day.

CHAPTER 17:
HOW TO CREATE A FUN ENVIRONMENT FOR YOUR CO-WORKERS AND EMPLOYEES AT WORK

Today, with a shrinking economy resulting in budget cut, lay-offs, and downsizing, morale in the workplace is at an all time low. So how can you create a low-cost way to make the office more fun for the employees who are still there? Here are some suggestions:

ADDING FUN TO EVENTS AND MEETINGS

- Invite employees to bring dishes to a potluck for lunch or an office party or picnic, and suggest a theme to make things more festive. For example, invite employees to bring their specialties to an ethnic foods night or to participate in a cooking contest, such as a bake-off or chili cook-off, with employees voting on their favorite dishes, and a novelty prize for the winner.
- Start off your meetings with a fun opener and add some humorous or inspirational touches to your meetings. For example, share a quick joke, particularly one related to the workplace or your industry, or bring in an inspirational quote or passage to read to begin the meeting. Or start the meeting by asking people to share something fun or inspirational that they did. For instance,

they might fill in a sentence such as: "My favorite way to have fun is…", "What I especially enjoy is…" or "One of the most fun things I did this past week (month, on the weekend) was…."

CREATING A MORE FUN WORK ENVIRONMENT

- Create a space in the office, where people can put up comments, short poems, cartoon favorites, and the like. This could be a bulletin board in the lunchroom, wall in a meeting room, or other location. Or post up long strips of wrapping paper along one wall, as one manager did, where people can write or draw whatever they want or tape on clippings from newspapers and magazines. Suggest a positive, motivational theme to use.
- Bring in a CD player or iPod, and invite people to bring in their favorite songs to play during lunch hour or on breaks. Then, employees can just listen or dance as they like, and some employees who are good at dancing might be invited to give others lessons.

INVITING EMPLOYEE SUGGESTIONS

- Create a fun box for the office, where employees can drop off suggestions on fun things to do. Then, go through these suggestions and implement those you like best. Or read these suggestions aloud at a meeting and invite employees to vote on those they like best and implement those. Even if suggestions are off the wall and impractical, read them aloud, too – always good for a laugh.

OTHER BOOKS BY THE AUTHOR

Here are other books on achieving success or improving work relationships by the author:

- *WANT IT, SEE IT, GET IT! VISUALIZE YOUR WAY TO SUCCESS*
- *ENJOY: 101 LITTLE THINGS TO ADD FUN TO YOUR WORK EVERYDAY*
- *30 DAYS TO A MORE POWERFUL MEMORY*
- *DISAGREEMENTS, DISPUTES, AND ALL-OUT WAR*
- *A SURVIVAL GUIDE FOR WORKING WITH HUMANS*
- *A SURVIVAL GUIDE FOR WORKING WITH BAD BOSSES*
- *A SURVIVAL GUIDE TO MANAGING EMPLOYEES FROM HELL*

AUTHOR CONTACT INFORMATION

Here's how to contact the author for information about other books and about speaking for your organization or putting on workshops and seminars for your organization:

Gini Graham Scott, Ph.D.
Director
Changemakers
425 Broadway, #115
Santa Monica, CA 90401
(310) 943-7541; Fax: (310) 451-1260
changemakers@pacbell.net
www.ginigrahamscott.com

Or visit Gini Graham Scott's Websites for her books:

www.workwithgini.com (books on improving work relationships)
www.wantitseeitgetit.com (featuring *Want It, See It, Get It!*)
www.enjoythebook.com (featuring *Enjoy! 101 Little Ways to Add Fun to Your Work Everyday*
www.badbosses.net (featuring *A Survival Guide for Working with Bad Bosses)*
www.workingwithhumans.com (featuring *A Survival Guide for Working with Humans, A Survival Guide to Managing Employees from Hell,* and *Disagreements, Disputes, and All Out War)*